n

7

Whenever I go and give talks about my books, children always ask me lots of questions. They want to know how old I am and how much money I earn. They ask what football team I support and whether I've got any pets. One little boy even asked what time I was allowed to stay up to at night!

At each session there's always one child who says to me 'Why do you write children's books?' There are many answers to that question. I write because I can't help imagining characters and inventing their stories. gives me great satisfaction finding e right phrases and plaiting together strands of the plot. I write to fulfil self and hopefully entertain my ders. I want to involve children, ake them laugh, maybe even them cry.

I'm also tremendously touched if children tell me that a book of mine has helped them through a troubling experience. If you're anxious or unhappy, it's so reassuring to read about someone else going through something similar. You feel you're not alone, that there's a friend who understands.

Partnership for Children is a wonderful organisation working internationally to help small children with their emotional development. Together with Booktrust, they have compiled this excellent booklet of reading suggestions. I hope that parents and carers can cuddle up with a worried child and read together. Books obviously can't always solve problems, but they're certainly an immense comfort and solace in times of stress.

Jacqueline Wilson

No Matter What

Author Debi Gliori
Illustrator Debi Gliori
Reading age 6+
Interest level 3+

Review 'I'm a grim and grumpy little Small and nobody loves me at all' says a little fox to his mother. In this beautifully illustrated picture book, Debi Gliori cleverly depicts the worries of a small child, which are laid to rest by the mother fox assuring him of her unconditional love.

With simple rhyming phrases and humorous illustrations, the story shows how, whatever happens, the mother will always love her child – 'no matter what'.

Publisher Bloomsbury Children's Books
Published 2003
Price £5.99
ISBN 0747563310

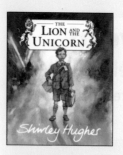

The Lion and the Unicorn

Author Shirley Hughes
Illustrator Shirley Hughes
Reading age 7+
Interest level 7-11

Review Evacuated during the Second World War, Lenny takes with him a badge given to him by his father, depicting a lion and a unicorn fighting.

Lenny is bullied by the children at his new school, but draws courage from his father's badge, and comes to terms with his fear and loneliness when he befriends Mick.

This remarkable story is masterfully written and accompanied by stunning illustrations.

Publisher Red Fox
Published 2000
Price £8.99
ISBN 0099256088

Angry Arthur

Author Hiawyn Oram
Illustrator Satoshi Kitamura
Reading age 5+
Interest level 5-8

Review A brilliantly illustrated book about a small boy's escalating rage when he is told that it's too late to watch television. His anger mounts and mounts, culminating in a 'universequake'! And at the end of the story, Arthur can't remember why he was so angry in the first place.

Although it looks a bit dated now (it was first published in 1982), this is an excellent book that can be used to discuss anger with young children – or just a good story that can be read and enjoyed for itself.

Publisher Red Fox
Published 1993
Price £4.99
ISBN 0099196611

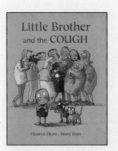

Little Brother
and the Cough

Author Hiawyn Oram
Illustrator Mary Rees
Reading age 6+
Interest level 3-8

Review In this excellent depiction of sibling rivalry, a little girl develops a noisy, disruptive cough which seems to get worse whenever her new baby brother is mentioned.

Finally, people begin to notice the cough, and with a bit of love and attention, it disappears!

The humorous illustrations work well with the text to make a charming book about a common problem.

Publisher Frances Lincoln Children's Books
Published 2000
Price £5.99
ISBN 0711208452

DIFFICULT FEELINGS

DIFFICULT FEELINGS

The **Feel Good** Book

Author Todd Parr
Illustrator Todd Parr
Reading age 4-8
Interest level 3+

Review This jolly little book uses simple sentences and uncluttered pictures with fat outlines and bold, vibrant colours to give its cheerful message. Some of the items will make adults smile, such as 'Brushing your hair with a lion feels good'. 'Watching your grandma and grandpa dance feels good' is illustrated by a wonderfully wacky pair of grandparents.

A great book to send children to bed with a warm glow, and a good starting point for further discussion about what makes you and your child feel good.

Publisher Little, Brown
Published 2002
Price Available on amazon.co.uk
ISBN 0316072060

The **Winter Dragon**

Author Caroline Pitcher
Illustrator Sophy Williams
Reading age 6+
Interest level 4-8

Review When Rory makes a toy dragon one winter, he finds that his new friend can come alive. The dragon protects Rory, in the early winter darkness, with his gleaming skin and shining eyes.

When spring comes it is time for Rory to say goodbye to his friend, but his warm memories keep him safe for winters to come.

This is an enchanting story, showing how a small boy uses his toy, his imagination and his memory to cope with anxiety and fear of the dark.

Publisher Frances Lincoln Children's Books
Published 2005
Price £5.99
ISBN 0711221864

Augustus
and his Smile

Author Catherine Rayner
Illustrator Catherine Rayner
Reading age 3+
Interest level 2+

Review Augustus is a tiger who,
though large and fearless, is sad
because he has lost his smile. He
goes on a journey to find it, but
despite looking everywhere, he fails.
Only when he finds a puddle and
sees his smile staring back from his
reflection, does he realise that he
will always have his smile, whenever
he is happy – and that happiness
can come from very simple things.

The adventurous artwork won
this book the 2006 Booktrust
Early Years Award for Best New
Illustrator. Although the story
appears very simple, it could be the
perfect prompt for getting children
to start talking about feelings.

Publisher Little Tiger Press
Published 2006
Price £5.99
ISBN 1845062835

Where the
Wild Things are

Author Maurice Sendak
Illustrator Maurice Sendak
Reading age 6+
Interest level 3+

Review This classic of children's
literature cleverly depicts how a
naughty boy goes to bed without
his supper, and in his anger goes
on a fantastical journey to a place
of wild monsters. As he tames
the monsters, he realises that
he wants to go back to 'where
someone loved him best of all'.

This book won the Caldecott Medal
for the Most Distinguished Picture
Book of the Year in 1964, and
has been delighting children and
parents ever since.

Publisher Red Fox
Published 2000
Price £5.99
ISBN 0099408390

DIFFICULT FEELINGS

Wanda's First Day

Author Mark Sperring
Illustrators The Pope Twins
Reading age 7+
Interest level 5-8

Review It's Wanda's first day at school and she is excited, yet nervous. On arriving, Wanda discovers she's the only witch in a class of fairies and worries whether she'll fit in. However, despite the fact that she is different, Wanda discovers that she enjoys her first day and looks forward to going again.

This is a clever take on the familiar story of first day nerves.

Accompanied by beautiful illustrations absolutely bursting with vibrant colour and detail, this book can't fail to delight little girls everywhere.

Publisher Chicken House
Published 2005
Price £5.99
ISBN 1904442523

Frog is Sad

Author Max Velthuijs
Illustrator Max Velthuijs
Reading age 5+
Interest level 4-8

Review Frog wakes up one day feeling sad, for no obvious reason. His friends try to cheer him up, but with no success. The Rat's violin playing makes him cry, and suddenly he can start to laugh again.

A gentle, sensitive book about changing moods that will strike a chord with many young children and their parents.

Publisher Andersen Press
Published 2005
Price £4.99
ISBN 1842704273

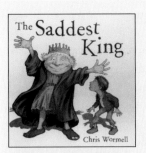

Let's Be Friends Again!

Author Hans Wilhelm
Illustrator Hans Wilhelm
Reading age 5+
Interest level 4-8

Review In a story that will ring true with many families, a boy's younger sister unwittingly does something that makes him terribly angry. He learns to deal with his fury, however, and finds that forgiveness and friendliness help not only his sister, but the boy himself, to feel better.

The book has charming illustrations (with an appealing dog!) and an optimistic message on resolving sibling conflict.

This title is now out of print. However, the entire book is downloadable, free of charge, from the author's own website: www.ChildrensBooksForever.com.

The Saddest King

Author Chris Wormell
Illustrator Chris Wormell
Reading age 5+
Interest level 5+

Review The king has decreed that everyone must be happy, so the people smile all day long, even when bad things happen. One day, a small boy is found crying, so he is sent to the king to be punished. As the boy tells the king the reason for his sadness – his dog has died – the king begins to sob, and his smiling face is found to be a mask. Thanks to the boy, the king realises it's all right to be sad sometimes, and revokes his decree, at which point everyone has a good cry!

Appealing illustrations of medieval-style villagers complement this story, which shows it's acceptable to express sadness and 'to be the way you feel'.

Publisher Red Fox
Published 2008
Price £5.99
ISBN 009948384X

Laura's Star

Author Klaus Baumgart
Illustrator Judy Waite
Reading age 7+
Interest level 3-8

Review Laura is lonely and has no-one to tell her special secrets to. But as she looks out of her bedroom window, a streak of silver comes twisting towards her, and she sees that it's a star.

She takes the shining star to her bedroom, repairs its broken point and tells it all her secrets.

This delightful story of friendship and compassion is a magical tale, ideal for bedtime reading.

Publisher Little Tiger Press
Published 2000
Price £5.99
ISBN 1854306960

The Not So **Abominable Snowman**

Author Matt Buckingham
Illustrator Matt Buckingham
Reading age 6+
Interest level 4-7

Review Bert is not your average abominable snowman. He doesn't just stay in the snowy mountains, but rather, he likes to run, jump, and chase butterflies in forests below. When Bert finds a little boy, Tom, looking for his father, he decides to help.

When Tom's father is eventually rescued by Bert and his friends, Tom realizes that maybe abominable snowmen aren't that abominable after all.

A charming story with quirky, colourful illustrations, this book is perfect for reading aloud to a young and imaginative audience.

Publisher Little Tiger Press
Published 2005
Price £5.99
ISBN 1845061993

Something Else

Author Kathryn Cave
Illustrator Chris Riddell
Reading age 6+
Interest level 4-8

Review Something Else is a lonely creature, excluded from everything because he is different. One day an equally curious creature (Something) turns up, giving him the chance to meet someone even stranger than himself.

At first he rejects him on the grounds that he is so peculiar, but then realises that this is exactly what he has experienced. This is the perfect book for reassuring any child that being different can be a very positive thing, and that people who are different can be friends.

Publisher Puffin
Published 1995
Price £4.99
ISBN 0140549072

Melrose and Croc
Friends for Life

Author Emma Chichester Clark
Illustrator Emma Chichester Clark
Reading age 4+
Interest level 3+

Review Croc is green and Melrose the dog is hairy. Croc is also helpful and enjoys playing noisy music. Melrose is good at somersaults but can be quite messy.

Through contemplations such as: Who am I? Who are you? I wish I were… I wish you were… and, I like the way you… the book explores the idea that people are unique, with different talents, interests and personalities. And in doing so it beautifully introduces the idea of learning to love others and yourself.

Publisher HarperCollins
Published 2006
Price £5.99
ISBN 0007182428

FRIENDSHIP AND DIFFERENCE

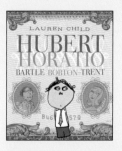

Melrose and Croc
Find a Smile

Author Emma Chichester Clark
Illustrator Emma Chichester Clark
Reading age 4+
Interest level 3+

Review Melrose and Croc are back, but Melrose is decidedly melancholy. He's lost his smile and, as any best friend should, Croc is anxious to help him retrieve it.

They take a drive to the country. Eventually, when Croc asks exactly what they were looking for, Melrose can't remember and… smiles!

The illustrations and text in this story of friendship have an airy, elegant simplicity accompanied by real emotional depth. The humour is perfectly judged, as is Melrose and Croc's St Tropez lifestyle and Croc's natty pink scarf!

Publisher HarperCollins
Published 2006
Price £5.99
ISBN 0007182411

Hubert Horatio
Bartle Bobton-Trent

Author Lauren Child
Illustrator Lauren Child
Reading age 7+
Interest level 6-10

Review Hubert Horatio Bartle Bobton-Trent, or 'H' for short, lives with his very rich parents in an enormous house.

When he begins to realise that his parents have squandered all their money, genius H and best friend Stanton Harcourt set out to find a solution to their financial crisis. In the end, they find that they don't need a lot of money to be happy.

Hilarious detail and fantastic illustrations make this picture book a real joy from start to finish.

Publisher Hodder Children's Books
Published 2005
Price £6.99
ISBN 0340877890

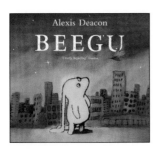

Beegu

Author Alexis Deacon
Illustrator Alexis Deacon
Reading age 6+
Interest level 4-7

Review Beegu is from another world and somehow gets lost on Earth. Lonely and confused, she wanders off to a nearby city to find some friends. But the only friendly people she comes across are the children, while the big Earth creatures just don't seem to understand.

The simple text and bold and enchanting illustrations cleverly convey a child's feelings of uncertainty and confusion when faced with new surroundings.

This is a heart-warming and satisfying tale that is certain to provide comfort to young children.

Publisher Red Fox
Published 2004
Price £5.99
ISBN 0099417448

Crispin:
The Pig Who Had It All

Author Ted Dewan
Illustrator Ted Dewan
Reading age 4-8
Interest level 4-8

Review This humorous yet heart-warming tale is of a young pig who, although given everything he ever asks for, is bored and lonely, as he quickly tires of his new toys.

His life is transformed when his new friends introduce him to the joys of imaginative play, where the fun is restricted only by the limits of their imaginations.

The detailed illustrations are warm and magical, and there is much to see in this vivid picture book for children aged 4 to 8.

Publisher Corgi Children's
Published 2001
Price £4.99
ISBN 0552546275

FRIENDSHIP AND DIFFERENCE

FRIENDSHIP AND DIFFERENCE

Queen Munch and Queen Nibble

Author Carol Ann Duffy
Illustrator Lydia Monks
Reading age 7+
Interest level 6-9

Review This tale of two very different queens, beautifully written and illustrated, is also great fun. Queen Munch is big and loud and colourful. She loves eating and, every Saturday morning, her subjects gather to watch the public Munching of the Breakfast.

In contrast, Queen Nibble is tall and slender and pale as a stick of celery. She spends most of her time alone, making jewellery from raindrops. But when Queen Munch invites her to stay, Queen Nibble has no choice but to go - and both queens find out how being different can form the basis for a great friendship.

Publisher Macmillan Children's Books
Published 2003
Price £6.99
ISBN 0333960661

Looking after Louis

Author Lesley Ely
Illustrator Polly Dunbar
Reading age 7+
Interest level 5+

Review Louis has an autistic spectrum disorder and reacts differently from his classmates. They have to learn how to understand him and help him to join in with their lessons and games. Initially disconcerted by his behaviour, they all find their own special pleasure when he shows he likes playing football, and they learn that sometimes you are allowed to break the rules for special people.

Completed by a simple professional explanation of the condition, the story sympathetically addresses some of the difficulties involved in dealing with autism.

Publisher Frances Lincoln Children's Books
Published 2005
Price £5.99
ISBN 1845070830

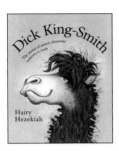

Hairy Hezekiah

Author Dick King-Smith
Illustrator John Eastwood
Reading age 8+
Interest level 5+

Review Hairy Hezekiah is a camel living a sad solitary life in a zoo, and seems to be the only animal without a friend. So he slips through the main gates to look for a mate.

Creating mayhem in the countryside as he searches, Hezekiah eventually reaches a safari park, where an instant rapport with the hirsute aristocratic owner results in the arrival of Hephzibah to share his life.

An appealing story about finding friendship from the author of 'Babe' and many other animal stories.

Publisher Young Corgi
Published 2006
Price £4.99
ISBN 0552552569

I'm Special, I'm Me!

Author Ann Meek
Illustrator Sarah Massini
Reading age 4+
Interest level 4+

Review Milo is a rather unconfident boy who is easily dominated by his schoolfriends - they never let him play what he'd like to be at playtime.

Each night his mother shows him another side of himself, until soon he has the confidence to be himself, and leads a game that all the other children are desperate to join.

Illustrated with warmth and joy by Sarah Massini, this is a new look at an old subject, and shows that inside every timid child is a happy one waiting to be brought out.

Publisher Little Tiger Press
Published 2006
Price £5.99
ISBN 1845060431

FRIENDSHIP AND DIFFERENCE

Whiff

Author Ian Whybrow
Illustrator Russell Ayto
Reading age 6+
Interest level 3-8

Review Whenever Whiff, the baby warthog, tries to make friends, it ends in disaster, as his lingering smell and the permanent cloud of flies always cause problems!

This comical, vibrantly illustrated picture book looks at the difficulties of making friends and the rewards of true friendship when you find it.

Publisher Picture Corgi
Published 2000
Price £4.99
ISBN 0552546151

Fox

Author Margaret Wild
Illustrator Ron Brooks
Reading age 7+
Interest level 7+

Review When she is lured away from Dog, her true companion and friend, by cunning Fox, who eventually abandons her far from home, Magpie learns the true value of friendship.

Accompanied by Ron Brooks' richly-coloured and textured illustrations, which create an expressive visual accompaniment to the dark narrative, this is a haunting picture book for children aged seven and over.

Publisher Allen & Unwin
Published 2008
Price £6.99
ISBN 1864489330

Camille
and the **Sunflowers**

Author Laurence Anholt
Illustrator Laurence Anholt
Reading age 7+
Interest level 5-8

Review Focusing on a short period in Vincent Van Gogh's life, this story is told through the eyes of Camille, the postmaster's son. His family befriends the artist and Vincent paints their portraits.

Not only do we learn about Van Gogh's paintings, but we also get an insight into the position of an 'outsider' in society.

The story covers themes of teasing and bullying by children and adults.

A short biography of the artist is included.

Publisher Frances Lincoln Children's Books
Published 2003
Price £5.99
ISBN 0711221567

Who's a **Big Bully Then?**

Author Michael Morpurgo
Illustrator Joanna Carey
Reading age 7+
Interest level 7+

Review Although written for 8-12 year-olds who have problems with reading, this is a great story for able 7-8 year-olds to read for themselves.

It tells of how a boy beats the school bully in a race – and the bully then wants a fight. The hero devises a clever trick to play on him, but at the end gets quite a surprise himself.

An engaging book by a master story-teller, with a twist in the tale.

Publisher Barrington Stoke
Published 2001
Price £4.99
ISBN 1842990179

BULLYING

Hugo and the Bully Frogs

Author Francesca Simon
Illustrator Caroline Jayne Church
Reading age 5+
Interest level 4+

Review Hugo is a little frog with a tiny croak, whose life is made miserable by some big, bad bully frogs.

The other animals suggest ways in which Hugo can defend himself, but he is just too timid.

Then, when bossy old Duck arrives, she soon hits on the answer.

Publisher Gullane
Published 2000
Price £5.99
ISBN 1862335967

Cliffhanger and Buried Alive (published together as Jacqueline Wilson's Biscuit Barrel)

Author Jacqueline Wilson
Illustrators Nick Sharratt and Sue Hea
Reading age 7+
Interest level 7-11

Review This edition brings together two of Jacqueline Wilson's funniest stories for younger children. 'Cliffhanger' sees Tim and his friend Biscuits reluctantly going on an adventure holiday, where Tim loathes the activities and feels he is failing at everything, but despite this ends up finding friendship and fun.

In 'Buried Alive', Tim and Biscuits go on holiday with Tim's parents to Wales, where all goes well until the arrival of two bullies, Prickle-Head and Pinch-Face. The story uses gentle humour to deal with issues of friendship and bullying (as well as embarrassing parents).

Publisher Corgi Yearling
Published 2001
Price £6.99
ISBN 0440864631

Bad Girls

Author Jacqueline Wilson
Illustrator Nick Sharratt
Reading age 8+
Interest level 7-11

Review Bitterly unhappy and fed up with being bullied at school, Mandy White is in need of a friend.

However, with her spiky orange hair, strappy stilettos and tendency to shoplift, the colourful Tanya isn't exactly what Mandy's parents would have wished for.

Bad Girls effortlessly depicts the sort of insecurities and concerns to which many young readers will surely relate.

Publisher Corgi Yearling
Published 2006
Price £5.99
ISBN 0440867622

There's a House Inside My Mummy

Author Giles Andreae
Illustrator Vanessa Cabban
Reading age 6+
Interest level 2-7

Review This is just the book to explain to inquisitive children what is going on inside mum during pregnancy.

Through a rhyming text, a toddler explains why his mum's tummy is getting so big, and what he expects to happen.

Soft, colourful pictures, full of domestic detail, contribute to the book's humorous approach, but also allow for discussion in greater depth, if desired.

Publisher Orchard Books
Published 2002
Price £5.99
ISBN 1841210681

No More Kissing!

Author Emma Chichester Clark
Illustrator Emma Chichester Clark
Reading age 5+
Interest level 3-7

Review Kissing drives Momo the monkey crazy, but unfortunately for him, his friends and family kiss each other at every opportunity. When his little brother is born, everyone kisses him too, but this doesn't stop his incessant crying.

Momo explains that obviously his little brother hates kissing too, and he tries to find other ways to stop him crying. He manages to placate the baby, and then unable to resist his brother's sweet smile, surprises himself by kissing him.

The book has adorable characters and a lovely unpredictable ending.

Publisher HarperCollins
Published 2002
Price £5.99
ISBN 0007131051

Crispin and the 3 Little Piglets

Author Ted Dewan
Illustrator Ted Dewan
Reading age 4-8
Interest level 4-8

Review The wealthy young pig from 'Crispin: The Pig Who Had It All' is here again. This time, he is shocked to discover that instead of one sibling (as expected), he has three! Inevitably, he gets pushed out of the limelight, but eventually, all ends well as the piglets win him over and he reads them a story – 'The Three Little Pigs'.

There is much to amuse adults as well as children in the fantastic, quirky illustrations (such as Crispin's mother on her exercise bike) which really bring the story to life and make this book special.

Publisher Corgi Children's
Published 2003
Price £5.99
ISBN 0552547864

My Mum's Going to Explode!

Author Jeremy Strong
Illustrator Nick Sharratt
Reading age 8+
Interest level 7-10

Review Nicholas is shocked when his mum announces she is pregnant. However, with the aid of Imelda (a one-legged, half-bald doll) and encouragement from Granny and her Hell's Angel husband, Nicholas and his father begin to prepare for the new arrival.

With short chapters and humorous line drawings throughout, this highly amusing tale is ideal for early readers.

Publisher Puffin
Published 2007
Price £4.99
ISBN 0141322360

I am Too Absolutely Small for School

Author Lauren Child
Illustrator Lauren Child
Reading age 6+
Interest level 3-7

Review Lola is nearly big enough to go to school. But in her opinion she is still really quite small, and has far too many important things to keep her extremely busy at home.

Lola's older brother Charlie tries to put his sister's mind at rest that school will be friendly and fun. And when she tries it, she finds – of course – that he is right.

This book is completely child-centred, from its subject matter to its illustrations, and will provide welcome reassurance for any children who are uncertain about this big step.

Publisher Orchard Books
Published 2004
Price £6.99
ISBN 1846168857

CHANGE - new baby/starting school

When an Elephant Comes to School

Author Jan Ormerod
Illustrator Jan Ormerod
Reading age 4+
Interest level 3-6

Review The first day at school can be as worrying for an elephant as it is for any child! Will they make any friends? What will they do all day? Will there be anything to eat? And what happens if they need the toilet ...?

This potentially anxiety-inducing topic is explored with both humour and reassurance with a clear, repetitive layout, detailed, humorous illustrations and gentle colour tones. This elephant will strike a chord with any school first-timer, personifying as it does their own anxieties – and hopefully allaying them.

Publisher Frances Lincoln Children's Books
Published 2005
Price £5.99
ISBN 1845074319

So What!

Author Bel Mooney
Illustrator Margaret Chamberlain
Reading age 8+
Interest level 7-10

Review This rather jolly little book offers a series of incidents in the life of 10-year-old Kitty and her family. Problems with homework, room tidying, and jealousy of a younger sibling, are dealt with in a fairly lighted-hearted way, but with sympathy for the difficulties of a child confronting the idea of 'growing up'.

The style of text and illustrations will appeal to quite young readers, and the topics covered could be usefully discussed both in a classroom situation and on a one-to-one basis.

Publisher Egmont Children's Books
Published 2002
Price £3.99
ISBN 0749748230

You'll Soon Grow Alex

Author Andrea Shavick
Illustrator Russell Ayto
Reading age 6+
Interest level 6+

Review Alex is unhappy with his height and desperately tries to grow taller. He receives much advice - drink plenty of milk, exercise, sleep and even read lots of books - but nothing seems to work.

Then Uncle Danny points out some of the drawbacks of being tall, and Alex realises there are more important things in life.

Superb illustrations bring this story alive.

Publisher Orchard Books
Published 2001
Price £4.99
ISBN 1841216062

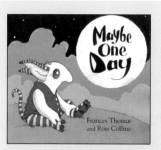

Maybe One Day

Author Frances Thomas
Illustrator Ross Collins
Reading age 6+
Interest level 4-8

Review Little Monster investigates the exciting explorations he would 'maybe' like to make when he's just a little bit older and ready to leave his parents.

With each suggestion, Father Monster voices some of Little Monster's own fears, but Little Monster gives rational responses to each, thereby enabling him (and the readers) to face and resolve these fears about growing up.

The brightly coloured pictures, while definitely extra-terrestrial, are filled with reassuring domestic detail.

Publisher Bloomsbury Children's Books
Published 2002
Price £4.99
ISBN 0747555699

CHANGE - growing up

Two of Everything

Author Babette Cole
Illustrator Babette Cole
Reading age 6+
Interest level 5-8

Review This quirky picture book follows the misfortunes of Demetrius and Paula Oglebutt who have problem parents.

The two children decide to take action and have the inspirational idea of organising an 'un-wedding'.

An extremely original, effective and comical approach to the difficult subject of divorce.

Publisher Red Fox
Published 2000
Price £5.99
ISBN 0099220628

Dinosaurs Divorce

Authors Laurene Krasny Brown and Marc Brown
Illustrators Marc Brown and Laurene Krasny Brown
Reading age 4+
Interest level 4+

Review This is not a story, but a book of practical information explaining why parents divorce, what children might feel about it and what might happen afterwards.

Illustrated with dinosaur characters, it has lots of reassuring, non-judgmental advice for children whose parents are splitting up and who may have to adapt to new family arrangements.

Publisher Little, Brown
Published 1993
Price £5.99
ISBN 0316109963

Amazing Grace

Author Mary Hoffman
Illustrator Caroline Binch
Reading age 7+
Interest level 5-8

Review This best-selling book has a great message for all children – you can be whatever you want, if you try. Grace is desperate to play Peter Pan in the school play, but she's told she can't because she's a girl, and because she's black. Fortunately, although her father is absent, Grace has a supportive mum and a wise Nana, who encourage her to go for her goals after all.

The astonishing illustrations complement an appealing and inspiring story. This book is also available in a number of dual-language editions: English-Urdu, English-Punjabi, English-Gujarati and English-Bengali.

Publisher Frances Lincoln Children's Books
Published 1993
Price £6.99
ISBN 1845077495

Grace and Family

Author Mary Hoffman
Illustrator Caroline Binch
Reading age 8+
Interest level 5+

Review In this sequel to 'Amazing Grace', Grace is invited by her father to visit him in Africa.

Grace's journey to The Gambia, and her attempts to come to terms with a newfound relationship with her father, a different culture and a large extended family, are sensitively and realistically portrayed.

Once again, the story is illustrated with stunning paintings by Caroline Binch.

Publisher Frances Lincoln Children's Books
Published 1995
Price £6.99
ISBN 1845078065

CHANGE - family break-up

Starring Grace

Author Mary Hoffman
Illustrator Caroline Binch
Reading age 8+
Interest level 7-10

Review There is no end to Grace's imagination! It is the school holidays and she and her friends spend their time playing at being everything from doctors to ghost-hunters.

Then when Grace takes part in her favourite musical 'Annie', she realises that what she really wants to be is a star!

This book tackles the subject of an absent father (who lives in The Gambia) and a mother's new boyfriend, with sensibility and great understanding of children's emotional needs.

Publisher Frances Lincoln Children's Books
Published 2003
Price £4.99
ISBN 0711221406

The Visitors who Came to Stay

Author Annalena McAfee
Illustrator Anthony Browne
Reading age 6+
Interest level 5+

Review Katy lives a quiet life by the sea with her dad, occasionally visiting her mum at weekends. Then one day, Dad brings home a friend and her son, and their loud and colourful ways totally disrupt her peaceful world. In time, it gradually dawns on her that these visitors are going to stay for good – because the woman is her dad's new partner.

This sensitive and sophisticated book, superbly illustrated by Anthony Browne (with plenty of visual jokes), explains a complicated and painful situation in a helpful and perceptive way.

Publisher Walker Books
Published 2000
Price £5.99
ISBN 0744567731

Good-Bye, Daddy!

Author Brigitte Weninger
Illustrator Alan Marks
Reading age 7+
Interest level 4-8

Review Tom is feeling sad after one of his father's regular visits.

So Teddy tells Tom a story of a little bear in a similar situation. Father and Mother Bear live apart, although Father Bear often comes to visit. Like Tom, Little Bear gets upset when he leaves.

Mother Bear explains that she and Father Bear used to argue a lot when they lived together, but now they are both happy and nothing changes their love for Little Bear.

A useful book for discussing separation with young children.

Publisher North-South Books
Published 2000
Price £4.99
ISBN 1558587705

The Suitcase Kid

Author Jacqueline Wilson
Illustrator Nick Sharratt
Reading age 8+
Interest level 7-12

Review Distraught at her parents' divorce, Andy cannot decide who she wants to live with. She spends one week at Mum's house, the next at Dad's, but never really feels that she belongs anywhere.

This difficult situation, which is worsened by animosity between Andy and her new stepfamilies, has no simple solution.

Approached with humour and understanding, this is a very readable tale of confusion, guilt and ultimately optimism, with which many children (and adults) will identify.

Publisher Corgi Yearling
Published 2006
Price £5.99
ISBN 0440867738

CHANGE - family break-up

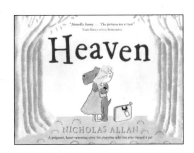

Heaven

Author Nicholas Allan
Illustrator Nicholas Allan
Reading age 6+
Interest level 4+

Review For Dill the dog, heaven is lampposts and meaty bones, while for his owner Lily it's islands of chocolate and ice-cream clouds. As Dill prepares to accept an invitation to heaven, readers are carefully prepared, through Lily's reactions, for a similar loss in their own life.

This book is outstanding for its delightful illustrations, gentle humour and perceptive grasp of the inevitably conflicting emotions and behaviour which frequently accompany bereavement.

Publisher Red Fox
Published 2006
Price £5.99
ISBN 0099488140

Granpa

Author John Burningham
Illustrator John Burningham
Reading age 4+
Interest level 3-8

Review Using a combination of gentle illustrations and minimal text, this is a sensitive and moving exploration of the relationship between a young girl and her grandfather.

In just a brief story, we get a sense of the grandfather's life and the little girl's reaction to his death.

And after he dies, she still has plenty of wonderful memories of him.

Publisher Red Fox
Published 2003
Price £5.99
ISBN 0099434085

Up In Heaven

Author Emma Chichester Clark
Illustrator Emma Chichester Clark
Reading age 6+
Interest level 3-7

Review Daisy the dog is devoted to her young owner Arthur, but now that she is very old she finds she cannot keep up with him anymore.

One night Daisy dies and goes to heaven, but she can see that Arthur misses her and is very sad. So she sends him comforting dreams telling him about heaven and how happy she is there, allowing him to finally move on, without forgetting her.

Beautifully illustrated, this is a gentle, unsentimental, yet comforting introduction to the difficult subject of death and bereavement for the very young.

Publisher Andersen Press
Published 2004
Price £5.99
ISBN 1842703331

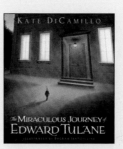

The Miraculous Journey of Edward Tulane

Author Kate DiCamillo
Illustrator Bagram Ibatoulline
Reading age 8+
Interest level 7+

Review Edward Tulane is an impressive and immaculate china rabbit. Abigail, his owner, adores and cares for him completely, but Edward does not return her love. Edward is self-centred, proud and heartless; he cares nothing for love.

Then, through a series of accidents, Edward is separated from Abigail. He learns about love, and experiences the pain that comes with loss and death. He wonders if he can bear to risk loving somebody.

This is an unusual, well-written and beautifully illustrated story. Edward's journey, both physical and emotional, is movingly told and full of vibrant characters.

Publisher Walker Books
Published 2008
Price £6.99
ISBN 1406307702

LOSS AND DEATH

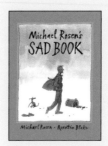

Always and Forever

Author Alan Durant
Illustrator Debi Gliori
Reading age 7+
Interest level 4+

Review When Fox dies, his family of Otter, Mole and Hare are plunged into grief and don't feel that life can continue without him. Then one day, Squirrel comes to visit, and they gradually remember the good times they had with him. They realise that 'in their hearts and their memories and their laughter' Fox will be there – 'always and forever'.

This is a moving and sensitive story, beautifully illustrated by Debi Gliori, which explains death gently and would be ideal for a young child facing a loss in the family.

Publisher Picture Corgi
Published 2004
Price £5.99
ISBN 0552548779

Michael Rosen's Sad Book

Author Michael Rosen
Illustrator Quentin Blake
Reading age 6+
Interest level 6+

Review The subject of bereavement is treated in an unusual way in Michael Rosen's Sad Book, which deals with the death of the author's own son.

The main character is an adult - Michael Rosen himself. Quentin Blake's illustrations sensitively complement an account of grief that is both searingly personal and reassuringly universal.

Publisher Walker Books
Published 2004
Price £10.99
ISBN 0744598988

Badger's Parting Gifts

Author Susan Varley
Illustrator Susan Varley
Reading age 7+
Interest level 4+

Review When Badger dies, his friends are very sad, but one by one they recall the special things he gave them during his lifetime.

By sharing these fond memories, they realise that although he is no longer with them physically, he will always be in their hearts.

A succesful book that deals gently and clearly with issues of loss and death for young children.

Publisher Picture Lions
Published 1994
Price £5.99
ISBN 0006643175

Frog and the Birdsong

Author Max Velthuijs
Illustrator Max Velthuijs
Reading age 7+
Interest level 3-8

Review Frog discovers a blackbird lying motionless on the ground.

He asks his friends what could be wrong and they eventually realise that the bird has died.

This picture book gently explains death to young children.

Publisher Andersen Press
Published 1999
Price £4.99
ISBN 0862649080

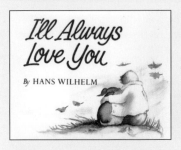

Grandma's Bill

Author Martin Waddell
Illustrator Jane Johnson
Reading age 7+
Interest level 4-8

Review Bill and his Grandma look through an album containing old photographs of Bill's grandfather, who is no longer alive.

A touching story about a young boy's special relationship with his grandparents.

Publisher Macdonald Young Books
Published 1991
Price £4.99
ISBN 0750003073

I'll Always Love You

Author Hans Wilhelm
Illustrator Hans Wilhelm
Reading age 6+
Interest level 4+

Review Charmingly illustrated with watercolour pictures, this book tells the story of the relationship between a boy and his dog, Elfie. As the boy grows taller, Elfie gets rounder and slower. One night, Elfie dies in her sleep. The boy is very sad, but it helps him to remember that he had told Elfie every night 'I'll always love you'.

This is a simple but very moving story of love for and loss of a pet, suitable for young children, but likely to bring tears to the eyes of readers of any age.

Publisher Crown Publications
Published 2002
Price Available on amazon.co.uk
ISBN 0517572656

LOSS AND DEATH

The Cat Mummy

Author Jacqueline Wilson
Illustrator Nick Sharratt
Reading age 8+
Interest level 7+

Review Mabel the cat is very special. She used to belong to Verity's mother, who died when Verity was born. One day Mabel goes missing; Verity searches for her but discovers that the cat has curled up and died at the bottom of her wardrobe.

After she learns at school that the Ancient Egyptians worshipped cats, she decides to mummify Mabel! However, Gran suspects that something is wrong, and Verity is very worried that she will not be able to keep her Cat Mummy secret for much longer.

A deceptively simple tale which explores the issue of bereavement for younger readers.

Publisher Corgi Yearling
Published 2002
Price £4.99
ISBN 0440864165

LOSS AND DEATH

BOOKTRUST

Booktrust

Thanks

Booktrust is an independent national charity that encourages people of all ages and cultures to discover and enjoy reading. The reader is at the heart of everything it does.

Its website contains thousands of children's book reviews, along with author interviews and teachers' resources.

Many of the reviews that appear in this guide are based on those on www.booktrustchildrensbooks.org.uk and we are indebted to Booktrust for its considerable contribution to this publication.

Booktrust runs a variety of schemes, projects and prizes and three national book-gifting programmes - Bookstart, Booktime and Booked Up.
Visit www.booktrust.org.uk to find out more.

The development of this booklet was made possible by a grant from The Dulverton Trust.

The costs of printing this edition have been shared by The Bernard Sunley Charitable Foundation, the students, staff and parents of Kingston Grammar School, Surrey, and the Christmas Yoga Classes in Farrington Gurney, Somerset.

The Persula Foundation is kindly paying for a copy to be sent to every public library.